BY
JOHN GUY

# WHO WERE THE ANCIENT ROMANS?

## HIGH STANDARD OF LIVING

As the Roman Empire grew, it became very wealthy. Money and treasures were brought in from abroad, along with slaves. The average Roman lived comfortably.

The process of ancient Rome becoming a power in the Mediterranean was long and slow. The lands were not united under a central political system. Instead, there were a number of independent city-states. Each city-state had a main town and several villages. The small city-state of Rome is said to have been created in 753 BCE. The people who lived there were Etruscan (from all over Italy) and Latin (from southern Italy). They all became known as Romans. From about 550 BCE, Rome was ruled by Etruscan kings, but in 509 BCE, the Romans drove the king out and Rome became a tiny, independent republic.

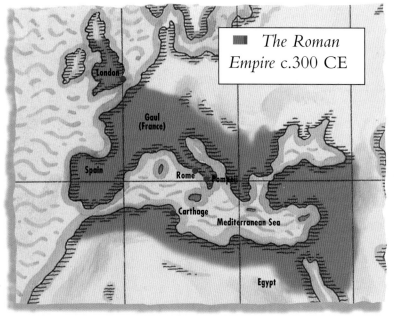

The Roman Empire c.300 CE

London

Gaul (France)

Spain

Rome

Pompeii

Carthage

Mediterranean Sea

Egypt

## A NIGHT ON THE TOWN

Most Roman towns had huge amphitheatres where they staged plays and sporting events. The Romans learned how to build a semicircular arch, which allowed them to build higher, more magnificent structures.

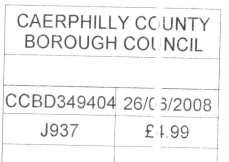

## THE MIGHT OF ROME

The strength and growth of the Roman Empire was due to its excellent army. The Romans organized a centrally controlled army, something no other civilization had managed to do.

## ROMULUS AND REMUS

According to legend, Rome was founded by twin brothers Romulus and Remus. Grandsons of the king of Alba Longa, and rejected by their parents, the twins were thrown into the river. They were saved by a she-wolf (shown here) and raised by a shepherd. When grown, the boys wanted to build their own city, and quarrelled about which hill to build on. Romulus ended up killing Remus, because he was angry at being teased about his small city walls. Romulus then crowned himeslf the first king.

## ORGANIZED SOCIETY

Roman society was very well organized. Young men learned a trade or joined the army; women created a stable family life.

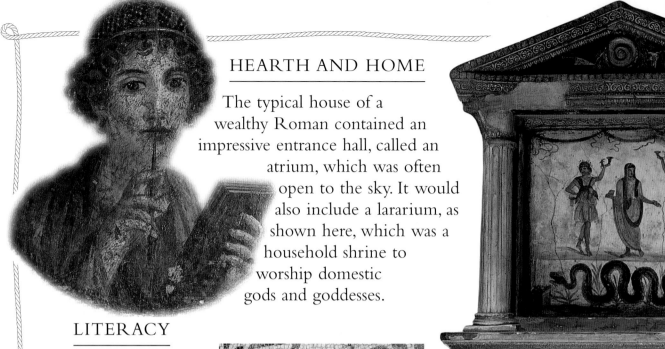

## HEARTH AND HOME

The typical house of a wealthy Roman contained an impressive entrance hall, called an atrium, which was often open to the sky. It would also include a lararium, as shown here, which was a household shrine to worship domestic gods and goddesses.

## LITERACY

Many nobles could read and write, having been educated by private tutors as children. The girl shown above is using a stylus to write on a wax tablet.

## HOME COMFORTS

Many of the richest Roman citizens had two houses, a town house and a country villa. Floors and walls were always cool, because they were made of marble or stone tiles, often inlaid with elaborate mosaics, as shown here.

## TAKING IT EASY

This elegant couch was used for afternoon naps. It would also have been used at mealtimes to seat two or three guests. Food would have been placed on low tables with several couches arranged around them.

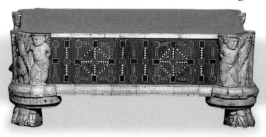

# LIFE FOR THE RICH

**W**hen we think of the Romans, we think about their luxurious lifestyle. However, it was only the very rich who lived so comfortably and had such beautiful possessions, some of which can be seen on these pages. The artworks and other items that have survived, belonged to the rich, and do not show us what life was like for the ordinary people. They are beautifully crafted and are made to a very high standard. They show how sophisticated Roman society was. In many areas, these high standards of living were not achieved again until the late 19th century.

## A STABLE SOCIETY

The Roman Empire, for a time at least, brought peace and stability to central and southern Europe, and with it came wealth for the ruling classes. Roman money was used throughout the empire, making trade easier.

## SLAVERY

Roman society made great use of slavery. Prisoners, captured from conquered lands, were put to work as labourers, or were employed as servants in wealthy households.

## THE FORUM

The central meeting place in a Roman town was called the forum, from the Latin word *foris*, which means 'outside'. It began as an open space where weekly markets were held.

# LIFE FOR THE POOR

There were great extremes in Roman life. The Roman Empire was one of the richest ever known. However, for most people life was very hard. It cost a lot of money to maintain the empire and taxes were very high, for rich and poor alike. The poor were jealous of the rich and their wonderful lifestyles. There was no system of care for the poor, and their lives were a constant struggle for survival. It was difficult to escape from poverty. Young men could enter the priesthood or join the army, so they had regular work.

## HOME COMFORTS

The poor had few comforts or luxuries. Their housing was very basic, and there was no sanitation. There were public baths, but few people could afford to use them.

## LIFE IN THE TOWNS

In the towns, most poor people lived in cramped, low-quality, shared housing. Few people in towns grew their own food; they bought their supplies from country people. Townspeople usually earned their living providing a service or trade.

## LIFE IN THE COUNTRY

Most country people were poor, just managing to make a living on small family farms. Cows were kept for their milk, poultry for eggs. Meat was rarely eaten. All members of the family worked, including the children. The men looked after the livestock, and did the heavy jobs, such as ploughing.

## SUBSISTENCE FARMING

Roman farming methods were quite basic, though by the standards of their day, Roman agriculture was better than that of most other Mediterranean countries. The Romans invented a new sort of plough, using a strong metal blade instead of a wood or bone one. It was able to cut a deeper furrow – very important when farming in the poor soils.

## FAMILY LIFE

Family life was very important to the Romans, both rich and poor. There were no pensions, so the whole family had to look after elderly relatives.

# FOOD AND DRINK

It is thought that Romans of all classes ate and drank well. Their food was probably very similar to the food that is eaten in the Mediterranean today. They enjoyed fresh fruit and vegetables, and would have eaten fish and poultry, too. Red meat was rarely eaten. Salads were served at mealtimes, often as a garnish or decoration. The poor enjoyed better food than people living outside the Roman Empire. Their basic diet was bread and vegetables, and they had their main meal after they had finished work for the day. The rich used mealtimes to get together with friends and family.

## HERBS AND SPICES

Roman housewives would be familiar with many of the herbs, used by modern cooks, to add flavour to their meals, such as parsley, thyme and fennel. Spices, imported from the East, were often used to disguise the taste of rotten meat.

## SERVING VESSELS

Romans used a variety of vessels for serving and drinking wine. Jugs and wine cups were made out of pottery, bronze or glass, or even finely engraved silver.

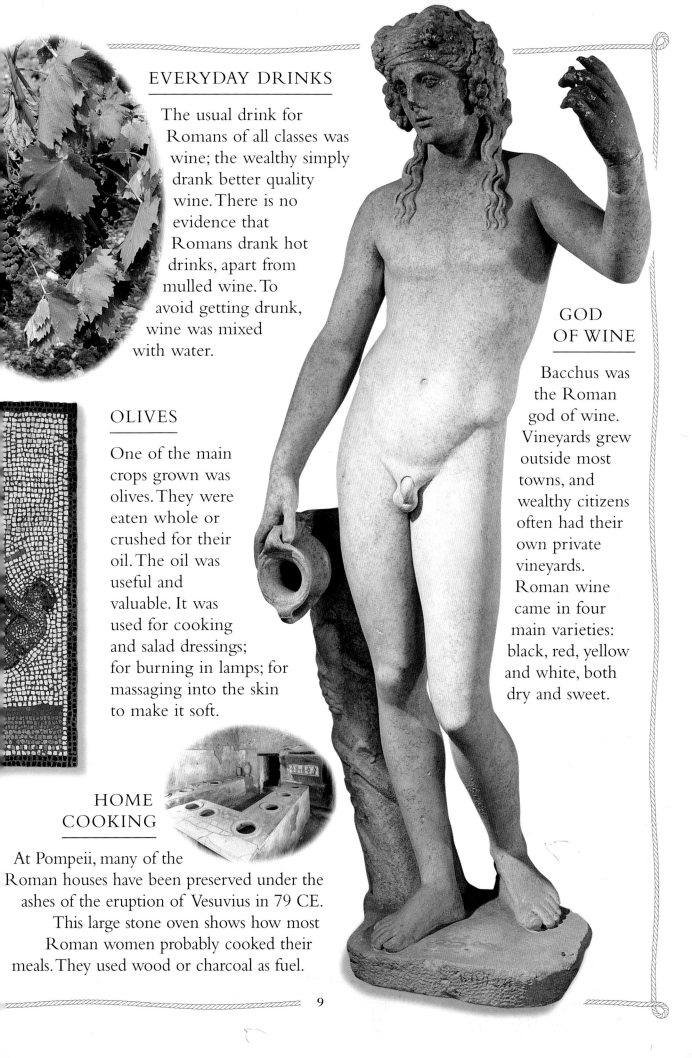

## EVERYDAY DRINKS

The usual drink for Romans of all classes was wine; the wealthy simply drank better quality wine. There is no evidence that Romans drank hot drinks, apart from mulled wine. To avoid getting drunk, wine was mixed with water.

## OLIVES

One of the main crops grown was olives. They were eaten whole or crushed for their oil. The oil was useful and valuable. It was used for cooking and salad dressings; for burning in lamps; for massaging into the skin to make it soft.

## HOME COOKING

At Pompeii, many of the Roman houses have been preserved under the ashes of the eruption of Vesuvius in 79 CE. This large stone oven shows how most Roman women probably cooked their meals. They used wood or charcoal as fuel.

## GOD OF WINE

Bacchus was the Roman god of wine. Vineyards grew outside most towns, and wealthy citizens often had their own private vineyards. Roman wine came in four main varieties: black, red, yellow and white, both dry and sweet.

## THE THEATRE

Romans were great theatregoers. Most towns had an amphitheatre, usually open to the sky, so most performances took place during the day. Only men could become actors.

## BLOOD SPORTS

Romans loved to watch blood sports. They usually went on all day. Wild animals, such as lions and tigers, were brought in to kill one another (at the opening of the Colosseum, 5,000 wild animals were killed in a single day).

## CHARIOT RACING

Most of the larger Roman towns had a stadium (a long arena) where chariot races were staged. Small, two-wheeled carts were pulled by two to four horses at great speed around a track.

## THE COLOSSEUM

The Colosseum in Rome was the greatest amphitheatre ever built. Unlike other theatres, it seems to have been designed for spectator sports, rather than for plays. Most amphitheatres were built into a natural dip in a hillside.

# PASTIMES

*E*ven working-class Romans, who spent most of their time working, enjoyed being entertained and going out. They went on theatre outings and visited the arena to watch sporting events. The Romans worshipped many gods, so there were feast days to celebrate, often with music and dancing. The rich preferred to hire musicians to play at their private parties, rather than join in public events. They also spent a great deal of time at the baths, where they met friends as well as enjoying the waters.

## AN EAR FOR MUSIC

Music was played at religious ceremonies and events at the arena. Only the poorer classes danced. Instruments were quite simple, such as flutes, panpipes and lyres (shown here).

## GLADIATORS

The most spectacular event at the Colosseum was watching the gladiators fight to the death.

# FASHION

## FOOTWEAR

Men and women wore sandals, which were comfortable in the hot sun. They came in various styles, but were usually flat or with very low heels. The thongs and straps were made of leather. The soles were made of shaped wood or heavy hide.

The Roman Empire lasted for nearly 700 years. Fashions changed during that time, as people developed new ideas and tastes over the generations. Both men and women liked to look good. Children did not have their own fashions, but wore miniature copies of adult clothes. As the climate was so hot, the most important matter was to keep cool. Light materials were therefore used. Those who could afford it bought expensive fabrics imported from abroad – silk from China and fine cotton from India. Light colours were used for clothes, including white. The colour purple was first chosen by the Romans as a symbol of power.

## MIRROR, MIRROR

Because the method of making mirror glass had not yet been mastered, the Romans made mirrors using highly polished pieces of metal.

## CHANGING FACE OF FASHION

Roman women liked their hair pinned back and held in place with a comb. It was fashionable for women to have pale skin, which was difficult in the Mediterranean sun.

## LOOKING GOOD

Women of all classes wore jewellery. Those who could afford it wore gold and silver necklaces, bracelets and earrings, decorated with jewels or rare stones. Bronze was used for cheaper pieces.

## THE TOGA

The toga was the national dress of Rome, and it was the right of all free-born citizens to wear it. However, the toga was normally worn only on special occasions and usually only by the rich. For normal, everyday wear, tunics were worn.

## FOLLOWERS OF FASHION

Early in Roman times, men had long hair and curly beards. By the end of the empire, a clean-shaven, cropped look was fashionable. Although fashion styles changed during the course of the Roman era, the basic design of clothes remained the same.

# ART AND ARCHITECTURE

## WALL PAINTINGS

Most Roman buildings, especially temples and the villas of the wealthy, were decorated with wall murals, usually showing scenes from mythology or the deeds of the gods.

The Romans copied, or adapted, many Greek architectural styles, adding their own details, and improving the designs. They used arches more than the Greeks, developing the semicircular arch. These techniques allowed the Romans to build higher and on a grander scale than had previously been possible. By adding a volcanic material called *pozzolana* (and other minerals) to their cement, they also created an incredibly strong type of concrete, stronger than the stones it bonded together. This meant masons could build strong walls much faster than before.

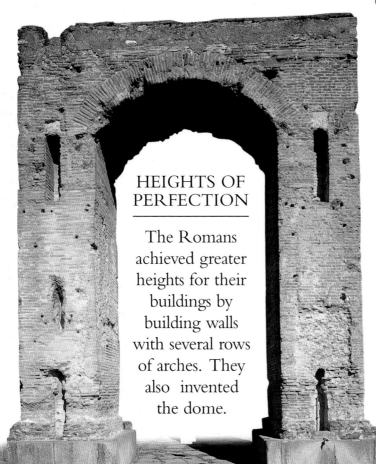

## HEIGHTS OF PERFECTION

The Romans achieved greater heights for their buildings by building walls with several rows of arches. They also invented the dome.

## MOSAICS

Many Roman buildings were decorated with mosaics on the floor or walls. They were very hard-wearing, and many have survived.

## FORTIFICATIONS

The Romans built massive fortifications to protect their empire, including strong city walls. The Emperor Hadrian built a huge defensive wall right across Britain from east to west. It was 117 km long, 4.6 metres high, and 3 metres thick.

## TOOLS OF THE TRADE

These tools were used by a Roman stonemason and are similar to those still in use today. They were especially used to create detailed carvings.

## EPHESUS

The Roman remains at Ephesus in western Turkey are amongst the finest to be seen anywhere. Many of the civic buildings survived at Ephesus, including the library of Celsius, shown here.

# HEALTH AND MEDICINE

## ROMAN BATHS

Water supplies were very advanced, and were not improved on in Europe until the 19th century. Most towns had public water fountains, bath houses and toilets.

The Romans understood the importance of personal hygiene, clean water and drainage systems to prevent disease. However, their knowledge of medicine was limited. They were a superstitious people, who thought that diseases were a curse from the gods. Because of this, many people looked for supernatural cures, by visiting healing shrines or by carrying lucky talismans to ward off evil spirits. Most physicians were Greek and they used many herbal remedies, which were quite effective for most everyday illnesses. There were no cures for more serious problems. Surgery was basic, and there was no form of anaesthetic. Amputations were carried out, and most army legions had a doctor, who traveled with them to look after the injured. However, many people died after treatment from infections.

## HEALING HANDS

This detail from a wall mural shows Aeneas, a legendary war hero, having an arrow-head removed from his leg by a surgeon. Antiseptic ointments, made from herbs, such as thyme, were used.

## SURGEONS' TOOLS

This collection of surgical instruments was in use throughout the Roman period, and is quite like those still used up until the 19th century. It includes knives and scalpels for making cuts, hooks to move blood vessels and organs during an operation and spatulas for mixing and applying ointments or for internal examinations.

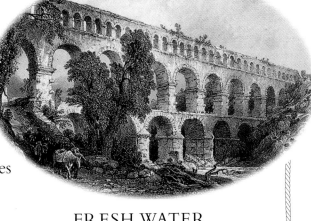

## FRESH WATER

The Romans could bring fresh water across deep valleys, as shown by this aqueduct at Nimes, in France.

## PERSONAL HYGIENE

This fragment of a hair comb is made of ivory. The relief shows a religious ceremony. It probably belonged to a rich person.

## NATURE'S CURE-ALL

The use of garlic for medicinal purposes had been widespread, probably since ancient Egyptian times. It was also claimed to have the power to remove evil spirits, so, to the Romans, it was really useful.

## CLEAN WATER SUPPLIES

The Romans developed a complicated system of water supply. They kept their drinking water away from drainage systems to prevent disease.

## CUPID'S ARROW

Cupid was the winged god of love. If Cupid fired an arrow into the hearts of a man and a woman they would fall in love.

## GOD OF FERTILITY

Bacchus the Roman god of wine, was also the god of fertility (after the Greek Dionysus). He is often associated with merry-making and wedding feasts.

## THE GODDESS OF LOVE

The Greek goddess of love and beauty was Aphrodite, whom the Romans renamed Venus. She is nearly always shown naked, or semi-clothed, as a beautiful young woman.

## THE WEDDING CEREMONY

This figurine shows the goddess Vesta giving her blessing at a wedding ceremony.

## GIRL POWER

This detail shows a young woman being accepted into priesthood. Unlike men who became priests and were allowed to marry, women priestesses were expected to remain unmarried.

# LOVE AND MARRIAGE

**M**any of today's marriage ceremonies and rituals can be traced back to the Romans. A plain wedding ring, for example, was placed on the third finger of the left hand because a nerve was thought to run from there directly to the heart. The bride wore a white toga with a coloured veil, and a feast was held at the house of the bride's father, where a wedding cake was served to the guests. Marriages were usually arranged between both sets of parents. Girls could be married as young as thirteen; boys were usually a little older.

## OBEDIENT WIVES

Women were expected to be dutiful wives and mothers. The more wealthy were allowed some freedom, but most were expected to obey their husbands.

## DEVOTED COUPLE

The Greek colony of Etruria in northern Italy played a large part in the founding of Rome. This Etruscan sarcophagus, comes from the tomb of a loving husband and wife.

# WOMEN AND CHILDREN

## MIDWIFERY

One of the few jobs that a woman could do was to be a midwife. Giving birth was dangerous and many babies and mothers died. The Romans are thought to have first performed a caesarean section.

Roman women had hard lives. They were treated as second-class citizens, and once married, became the property of their husband. The richer they were, the more freedom women could enjoy. However, most women were expected to run the house, look after the family, work in the fields and do the spinning and weaving, too. Only children from wealthy families were educated. They usually had a private tutor although some went to school. Girls were educated to a very low standard and then they were taught how to run a house and do other jobs, such as weaving. Boys were prepared for a profession, so spent longer with their tutor. Poor girls would either work in the fields or become servants.

## WORKING ON THE LAND

Most country people farmed their land and just managed to live on what they grew. Women and children did many jobs, which included sowing seeds, tending the crops, feeding the poultry and milking the cows.

## PLAYTHINGS

Children played with a variety of toys, and some were quite sophisticated. These pieces are from a game similar to dominoes.

## THE VESTAL VIRGINS

The cult of Vesta was especially linked with women. Her shrine and holy flame in Rome were attended by a small group of priestesses known as the Vestal Virgins.

## JUNO

The patron goddess of women was Juno, one of Jupiter's wives. She is normally shown seated, as in this fine terracotta statue. She was very motherly and protected women.

## SONG AND DANCE

Isis was an Egyptian god adopted by the Romans, and is particularly linked with women and children. This relief shows women and children dancing as part of a religious ritual to Isis.

## CHILDHOOD

This child wears a *bulla* (lucky charm) around his neck, which would have been given to him at a naming ceremony a few days after his birth. Only 50 percent of children were expected to reach 20.

# WAR AND WEAPONS

## AUGUSTUS

Caesar's adopted son Octavian (later known as Augustus) brought order to Rome after the civil wars of his father's time. He was a brilliant general and politician, and defeated Cleopatra.

From the 8th century BCE until about 509 BCE, Rome was ruled by its Etruscan neighbours in the north. When Rome became a republic in that year, the Romans chased the Etruscan king, Tarquin the Proud, out, and ruled themselves. Rome's power gradually grew to take control of most of Italy. Around 260 BCE, Rome argued with Carthage, a northern African state, and a century of bitter wars began. When Rome finally won in 146 BCE, it had gained its first overseas conquest. Rome's highly organized army then went on to conquer neighbouring lands.

## GALLEYS

Roman warships, known as galleys, were powered using sails and oars, with slaves as oarsmen. They had a huge battering ram on the bow (front) to ram enemy ships.

## HANNIBAL

Rome's second attempt to invade Carthage was stopped by Hannibal, a brilliant general who marched his army with forty war elephants across northern Africa, Spain, and across the Alps to Italy, to launch a surprise attack on Rome.

## PRIDE OF ROME

Roman legions consisted of about 5,000 infantrymen, and were the pride of the empire's army. They were helped by cavalry, who covered their flanks in an attack and scouted ahead, and by foot-soldiers, who manned the frontier forts, protecting the empire from attack.

## LEGIONNAIRES

The success of the Roman Empire was due to its highly organized fighting legions. Earlier civilizations, including the Greeks, and the Etruscans before them, did not manage to maintain a centrally organized army.

## JULIUS CAESAR

Civil war frequently broke out in the 'old' republic of Rome as generals competed for power. Julius Caesar (c.100-44 BCE) declared himself supreme dictator, but he was assassinated by his fellow senators.

## ROMAN WEAPONS

Roman weapons were usually made of iron or steel, with wooden or bone hand grips. Legionnaires were usually armed with a dagger and a sword. They used short-bladed swords with double-edged blades as a stabbing weapon. Foot soldiers also used throwing spears, short bows and javelins.

## SIEGE ENGINES

The most common form of Roman siege weapon was the *ballista*, as shown here. This large piece of military equipment could hurl a large boulder several hundred metres.

# CRIME AND PUNISHMENT

*T*he centre of Roman law-making was the Senate in Rome. Its members, the senators, were voted into office. They had long discussions about how the government should run the empire, but they were also influenced by the people, and sometimes made laws to gain popularity. The Romans introduced magistrates' courts where criminals were tried for crimes, including offences against the gods, and where people could bring their disputes. The guilty usually had to pay compensation rather than go to prison.

## THE NEW REPUBLIC

After the chaos of civil war, which led to the assassination of Julius Caesar, his adopted son, Augustus, had to restore order. He declared Rome a 'new' republic and became emperor.

## CRUCIFIXION

Crucifixion was a common form of execution in Roman times, and not just for religious victims. Death was slow and very painful. Usually the victim's arms were tied above his head onto a single pole; sometimes they were fastened to a cross.

## CORRUPTION

The Romans were proud of their fair and democratic constitution. However, laws were made or cancelled to gain public popularity. As the power of Rome began to fade, many senators began to take bribes from rich merchants.

## TRIAL BY COMBAT

Many people who were made to fight in the Colosseum (shown above) were criminals. The spectators liked to see them compete against wild animals and fierce gladiators.

## THE PRICE OF HOMAGE

It was usual for emperors, after a great victory, to be presented with captured children in homage, an act of respect. Many conquered people became slaves; any who refused to pay homage were executed.

## DEATH BY EXECUTION

The Romans were strict. Many crimes carried the death sentence, including stealing and treason. This illustration shows death by sword, axe and stoning.

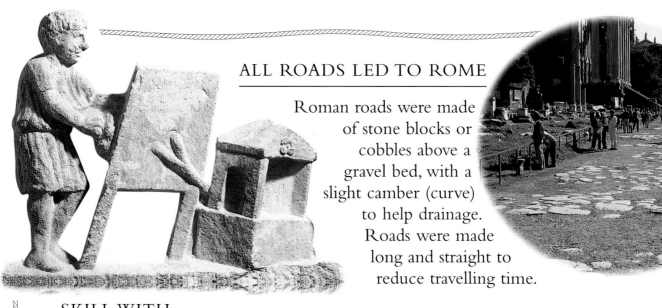

## ALL ROADS LED TO ROME

Roman roads were made of stone blocks or cobbles above a gravel bed, with a slight camber (curve) to help drainage. Roads were made long and straight to reduce travelling time.

## SKILL WITH METALS

The Romans were skilled metalworkers, making tools, weapons, utensils and fine jewellery.

## WIND POWER

Sailing in Roman times was dangerous and usually only attempted in good weather. Basic navigation relied on simple observation and movements of the moon, stars and planets.

## LIGHTHOUSES

The ruin of this Roman pharos (lighthouse) can still be seen on the cliffs at Dover Castle, Kent.

## ROAD TRANSPORT

Merchants used either pack animals or carts, pulled by oxen or horses, to take their goods to market.

# TRANSPORT AND SCIENCE

The Romans were good at developing new ideas, especially in technology. They realized that it was important to have a clean water supply to avoid diseases, so they developed a system of piping and drainage for their towns and villas. This led to the introduction of the plunge bath and the development of the hypocaust, a clever, under-floor central heating system. In architecture, the Romans invented a new sort of very strong concrete and improved the way bricks were made. They used arches to span greater distances than had been possible in earlier civilizations, and this led to the invention of the dome. But the greatest success of the Roman Empire was the network of roads they made.

## GREAT IDEAS

This view shows the ruins of the Roman baths at Carthage. It shows the hypocaust, where the floor was raised on pillars to allow hot air from furnaces to circulate.

## CENTRAL HEATING

The hypocaust was a system of central heating based on the fact that hot air rises. It both heated the water and warmed the rooms of private houses and public baths. This view shows how the system worked. Hypocausts were very popular in houses in the north, where it was colder in winter.

# RELIGION

*M*any of the gods in the Roman world were taken from ancient Greek mythology. The Romans simply renamed them. The Romans were superstitious and feared their gods. They made offerings to ward off evil spirits. As they took over new lands, the Romans also gained new gods and religious beliefs from the peoples they conquered. Romans who were posted to the outlying regions of the empire, such as Britain, often adopted their customs. Gradually, some Romans began to believe in the Christian God, whom they worshipped, as well as their own gods. By about 337 CE, Christianity had become the main religion of the Roman Empire.

## APOLLO

Unlike all the other gods, Apollo was known by the same name to both the Greeks and Romans. He was the god of the sun.

## MITHRAISM

Mithras was originally the Persian god of light, linked to the sun. Here we see him sacrificing a bull.

## GOD OF WAR

Mars was the Roman god of war and is usually shown as a powerful soldier wearing full armour. The month of March is named in honour of him.

## KING OF THE GODS

The most powerful of all the Roman gods was Jupiter. He was the god of light and the sky, symbolized by thunder and the eagle.

## FEMALE CULTS

A few Roman religions were associated with women only, such as Vesta. This view shows the temple of Vesta, in Rome.

## CATACOMBS

Although early Roman Christians may have used catacombs as a secret meeting place, they were originally a place of burial, the bodies being placed on ledges in the walls.

## GODDESS OF WISDOM

Minerva was the Roman equivalent of the Greek Athena and was the goddess of handicrafts and wisdom. She is often shown, as here, in a warlike pose, to symbolize the power of the empire.

## SACRIFICES

Sacrificial altars, where animals were killed, were usually placed outside the entrances to temples.

# ROMAN INFLUENCE

The Roman Empire is still influencing us today. Many modern European roads are built over old Roman ones. Modern plumbing and sewage systems are based on Roman ideas. Western architecture and language are also influenced by the Romans. Other aspects of Roman society, such as literature, military strategy and law, still affect us today. When studying the remains of Roman society today, it is easy to be misled. Almost all Roman remains are of the grand stone buildings, such as civic buildings and temples, because these have lasted better over the centuries. Roman society was rich and technologically brilliant, but we should try to imagine what life was like for ordinary people.

## ROAD BUILDING

One of the greatest things left behind by the Romans was their engineering skill, particularly in road-making.

## CLASSIC DESIGNS

Few whole Roman buildings survive, but British architects borrowed many classical designs for their buildings, especially in the 18th and 19th century.

## THE EMPIRE DIVIDES

By 476 CE, the Western Empire had fallen to invaders from the north. The Eastern Empire continued for another 1,000 years. Many of the Roman traditions remained, including architectural styles.

## THE FALL OF THE EMPIRE

In 406 CE, Germanic tribes overran the Rhine border in the north, and in 410 CE, Rome itself was sacked. The army was called back to defend Rome. But by 476 CE, the Western Empire had fallen.

## ATTILA THE HUN

Attila the Hun, from Central Asia, was a ruthless warrior, known as the 'scourge of god'. He extended his territory from the Rhine to China, and in 447 CE defeated the Roman Emperor Theodosius.

## MODERN EUROPE

The break-up of the Roman Empire was largely responsible for the formation of modern Europe. Turkey kept elements of both east and west, as it still does. This view shows St Sophia Mosque in Istanbul.

## UNIQUE SURVIVAL

The excavated city of Pompeii is a unique record of the Roman world. In 79 CE, the city, near present-day Naples, was destroyed when the volcano Vesuvius suddenly erupted. Modern excavations have found a city untouched by time, showing all aspects of everyday life.

# GLOSSARY

**Amphitheatre** An open-air theatre for watching plays and sports. Usually a circular or oval area of ground around which rows of seats are arranged on a steep slope.

**Amputation** To cut off part of the body. Usually done by a surgeon.

**Aqueduct** A structure for carrying water across land, especially one that looks like a high bridge with many arches.

**Catacomb** A series of underground passages and rooms where bodies were buried.

**Dictator** A leader who has complete power in a country.

**Execution** When someone is killed as a legal punishment.

**Homage** Deep respect and often praise shown for a person or god.

**Ruin** The broken parts that are left from an old building or town.

**Sacrifice** To kill an animal or a person and offer them to a god or gods.

**Siege** A military operation in which enemy forces surround a town or building, cutting off essential supplies. The aim is to take control.

**Superstitious** Having belief which is not based on human reason or scientific knowledge, but is connected with ideas about magic.

**Treason** The crime of betraying your country, especially by helping its enemies or attempting to defeat its government.

968 Pen

## ACKNOWLEDGEMENTS

We would like to thank: Graham Rich, Rosie Hankin and Elizabeth Wiggans for their assistance.
Copyright © 2008 *ticktock* Entertainment Ltd.
First published in Great Britain by *ticktock* Media Ltd., Unit 2, Orchard Business Centre, North Farm Road, Tunbridge Wells, Kent, TN2 3XF, UK.
All rights reserved. No part of this publication may be reproduced, stored in a retrieval system, or transmitted in any form or by any means electronic, mechanical, photocopying, recording or otherwise, without prior written permission of the copyright owner.
A CIP catalogue record for this book is available from the British Library.
ISBN 978 1 84696 663 7
Picture research by Image Select. Printed in China.

Picture Credits:
t=top, b=bottom, c=centre, l=left, r=right, OFC=outside front cover, IFC=inside front cover, IBC=inside back cover, OBC=outside back cover

AKG; London 10/11, 17br, 23ct, 24bl. Alinari - Giraudon, Paris; 7tl, 9cb, 14bl, 19tr, 31br. Ancient Art and Architecture; 18cl, 23cb, 22/23ct. Ann Ronan at Image Select; 7cr, 7cb, 17tr, 17bl, 22cb, 23r, 23b, 24tl, 26br, 26/27c, 26tr, 28l, 29br, 31tr & OBC. Archives Larousse - Giraudon; 10/11cb & OFC. Bridgeman Art Library; 16/17ct, 17cr, 27br. Chris Fairclough Colour Library / Image Select; 6cr, 15r, 16tl, 20bl, 30/31c. Corbis Bettman; OFC (main pic). et Archive; 24br. Gilles Mermet - Giraudon; 18/19ct, 22bl. Giraudon; 2/3cb, 2tl, 4c, 6b, 6tl, 8bl, 8cr, 10r & OFC, 12/13cb, 12tl, 14tl, 15tl, 16bl, 19b, 21tr, 21tl, 25b, 25t & IFC, 26tl, 26bl, 26/27c, 28c, 28b, 29tr, 30b. Image Select International; 2/3ct & OBC, 3br, 3tr, 5tr, 5cb, 9tl, 10tr & OFC, 10tl, 13br, 12/13ct, 12bl, 15br, 14/15b, 22tl, 29tl & OBC, 29c, 30/31c. Pix; 30tl. Spectrum Colour Library; 8tl. The Telegraph Colour Library; 30l. Werner Forman Archive; 5cr, 4tr, 4b, 4tl, 9r & OFC, 11tr, 13tr, 18tl & OBC, 18bl, 18c, 20tl, 20br, 21b, 25c, 27tr, 29cb.

Every effort has been made to trace the copyright holders and we apologize in advance for any unintentional omissions.
We would be pleased to insert the appropriate acknowledgement in any subsequent edition of this publication.